Foundations

LEVEL Cursive Workbook

Denise Eide

Foundations Level B Cursive Workbook by Logic of English

Pedia Learning Inc.
10800 Lyndale Ave S. Suite 181
Minneapolis, MN 55420

Cover Designer & Illustrator: Ingrid Hess
Royalty Free Images: Shutterstock
LOE School Font: David Occhino Design

ISBN 978-1-936706-34-1

First Edition

10 9 8 7 6 5 4 3 2 1

www.LogicOfEnglish.com

LESSON 41

41.1 Phonogram Desk Chart

Aa Bb Cc Dd Ee Ff

Hh Ii Jj Kk Ll Mm Nn

Oo Pp Qq Rr Ss Tt Uu Vv

Ww Xx Yy Zz

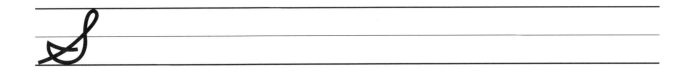

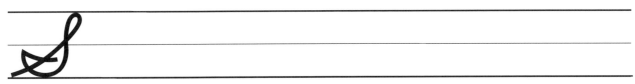

sh	y	x
v	f	k
h	b	l

t	g	w
x	sh	m
b	s	a

41.3 Tic-Tac-Toe continued

c	g	i
p	sh	o
j	y	v

z	y	w
a	qu	f
r	sh	x

fun hat

big logs

red brush

hands clap

fish swim

hut on sand

milk jug

trash can

plant wilts

red ship

LESSON 42

Name _____

42.1 Uppercase T

m	z
g	g
z	n
T	T
n	s
S	m

and	ask
best	drink
fast	help
jump	just
must	stop
that	them
think	this
wish	with
fish	hand

High Frequency Words

High Frequency Words

High Frequency Words

High Frequency Words

High Frequency Words

High Frequency Words

High Frequency Words

High Frequency Words

High Frequency Words

High Frequency Words

High Frequency Words

High Frequency Words

High Frequency Words

High Frequency Words

High Frequency Words

High Frequency Words

High Frequency Words

High Frequency Words

LESSON 43

43.1 Syllables and Pictures

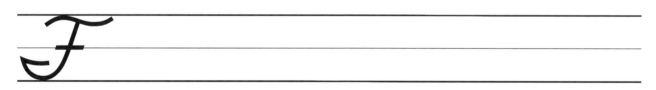

Name _____

we	did	wish
and	with	me
think	go	not

he	had	she
ran	no	yes
them	must	so

LESSON 44

Name _____

44.1 Uppercase H

He jumps.

She hits.

She thinks.

She jumps.

He hits.

She sits.

He runs.

He sits.

He thinks.

She runs.

LESSON **45**

45.1 Uppercase M

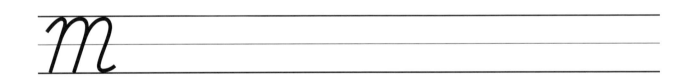

the	am	can
be	an	cut
help	and	his

ask	did	the
with	his	hot
best	him	at

REVIEW

Name _____

A.1 Long and Short Vowels

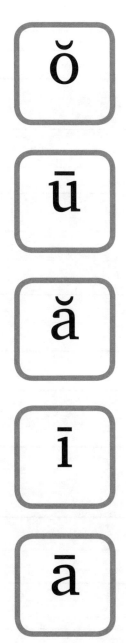

Name _____

$\mathscr{S}$ $\mathscr{T}$ $\mathscr{F}$ $\mathscr{H}$ $\mathscr{M}$

1. th   s   sh   t

2. th   t   w   g

3. b   d   v   f

4. k   x   t   sh

5. o   a   e   y

He is on the ship.

She runs fast with the dog.

He is sad.

She sits and thinks.

this

that

he

she

go

so

we

is

had

a

his

the

LESSON 46

46.1 Phonogram Flip

sh

th

M

H

T

S

F

z

w

N n 𝓝 𝓂

𝓃

𝓃

𝓃

𝓃

Sal has a clock.

The clock ticks and tocks.

Sal drops the clock.

Crash! Smash!

Sal is sad.

LESSON 47

47.1 Vowels

ă	ā
ĕ	ē
ĭ	ī
ŏ	ō
ŭ	ū

__ock

tr

s

br

cl

r

l

___ick

__ock

___uck

__ock

___ock

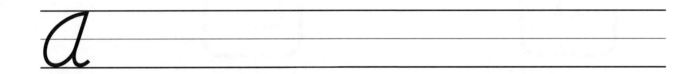

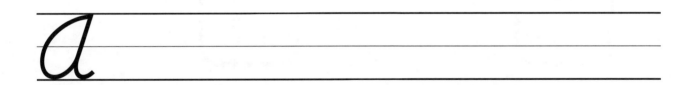

f	*m* (cursive)
m	*T* (cursive)
h	*a* (cursive)
t	*F* (cursive)
n	*H* (cursive)
a	*n* (cursive)

She naps.

The man is in the tent.

The man has a fish.

The sun is hot.

The frogs jump and hop.

The man is on the ship.

He hit the puck.

He lost his sock.

LESSON 48

Name _____

48.1 Uppercase D

$\mathcal{D}$

$\mathcal{D}$

$\mathcal{D}$

$\mathcal{D}$

| fr | br | tr | dr | thr |

| bl | fl | pl | cl | spl |

| gl | pr | cr | sl | spr |

48.3 High Frequency Word Game

a	be
go	he
his	is
stick	light
me	night
right	no
she	so
the	we
black	back

High Frequency Words

High Frequency Words

High Frequency Words

High Frequency Words

High Frequency Words

High Frequency Words

High Frequency Words

High Frequency Words

High Frequency Words

High Frequency Words

High Frequency Words

High Frequency Words

High Frequency Words

High Frequency Words

High Frequency Words

High Frequency Words

High Frequency Words

High Frequency Words

LESSON 49

Name _____

49.1 Uppercase B

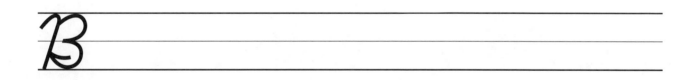

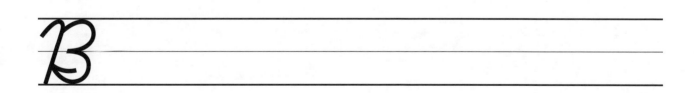

bl

sl

tr

dr

cl

sl

dr

spl

pl

cl

gl

black

slap

trap

drop

clap

slam

drip

splash

plan

click

glad

Six ducks swim.

Sam sits on the dock.

Sam has a snack.

The red duck quacks, "Snack, snack."

Sam drops his
snack. Splash!

The ducks swim
fast.

The ducks grab
his snack.

The ducks quack,
"Snack, snack."

LESSON **50**

Name _____

50.1 Uppercase P

$\mathcal{P}$

$\mathcal{P}$

$\mathcal{P}$

$\mathcal{P}$

1.   m   *m*   n   𝒩   𝓇   m   **M**

2.   t   *t*   l   w   𝒯   𝓕   t   **T**

3.   p   𝓈   𝒫   s   h   𝓅   **O**   **P**

4.   a   **A**   𝒶   𝒶   g   d   **o**   𝒹

5.   th   𝒯𝒽   th   sh   wh   𝓉𝒽

REVIEW **B**

Name _____

B.1 Long and Short Vowel Sounds

ĕ

ē

ĭ

ī

ŏ

Name _____

n a D B P

1. th | sh | igh | ch

2. ch | sh | wh | th

3. ch | ck | sh | igh

4. th | ck | igh | sh

5. sh th ck ch

6. igh th ck ee

Mom has three cats.

The pan is hot.

Frogs jump.

Drink the milk.

The black sheep sleep at night.

The chicks peck at the seeds.

She needs a bath.

LESSON 51

51.1 Uppercase R

R

R

R

R

1. M N *n* **m** n *m* N

2. S *S* d D **h** *s* **S**

3. T *f* j **t** *T* F t *H*

4. N *M* n *n* r *m* **M**

5. *a* R O o A *a* a

6. *R* **R** *P* g *r* r *B*

green	has
her	keep
much	pick
see	sleep
then	three
went	duck
feet	milk
nest	seed
sheep	tree

High Frequency Words

High Frequency Words

High Frequency Words

High Frequency Words

High Frequency Words

High Frequency Words

High Frequency Words

High Frequency Words

High Frequency Words

High Frequency Words

High Frequency Words

High Frequency Words

High Frequency Words

High Frequency Words

High Frequency Words

High Frequency Words

High Frequency Words

High Frequency Words

LESSON **52**

Name _____

52.1 Uppercase W

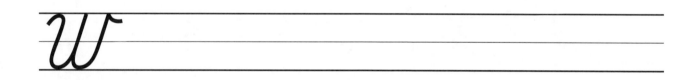

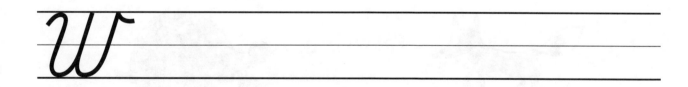

Name _____

1 2 3

1 2 3

1 2 3

1 2 3

1 2 3

1 2 3

Which bag is his?

The green bag is his.

Which cat is hers?

The black cat is hers.

Which gift is hers?

The green and red gift is hers.

Which pet is his?

The tan sheep is his.

LESSON **53**

53.1 Plurals

cat__

cat__

tree__

tree__

toy__

toy__

U u $\mathcal{U}$ u

$\mathcal{U}$

$\mathcal{U}$

$\mathcal{U}$

$\mathcal{U}$

tan packs ___   trees ___

toy truck ___   bus ___

rocks ___   hands ___

hats ___   boys ___

lights ___   street ___

steps ___   feet ___

LESSON 54

54.1 Long and Short Vowels

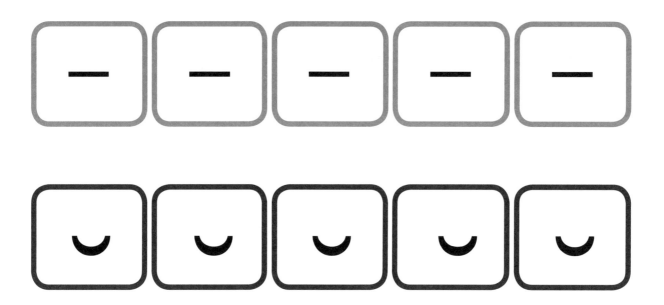

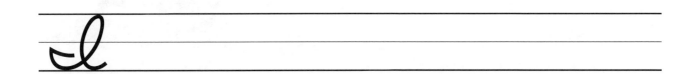

The cat has a black tail.

The pail is in the sand.

The cat has mail.

The fish jumps in the pail.

The coin drops in the bank.

The cat plays with the toys.

The toy pops up.

The ducks swim.

LESSON 55

55.1 Uppercase J

Name _____

j	F
i	J
r	I
f	D
b	R
d	B

55.3 Phonogram Boat Race

REVIEW C

C.1 Syllables

1   2   3

1   2   3

1   2   3

1   2   3

paint_

fin_

pan_

lock_

coin_

chair_

Name _____

R W U I J

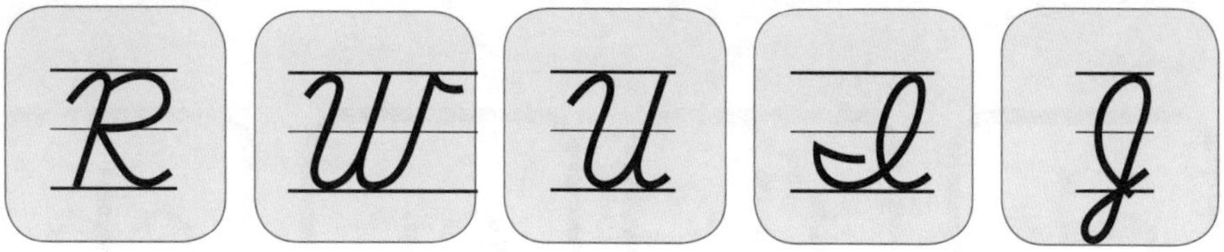

1. ck   th   er   ch

2. ee   er   oy   oi

3. ai   oy   ee   ay

4. ee   ai   igh   oi

5. wh   th   ch   sh

6. ai ee igh er

7. wh oy ch y

8. oy ay ai oi

9. er igh ai oi

10. oy ee er wh

She is in the light.

His pail is in the sand.

The kids play.

He has mail.

The boy has his light on.

She plays with the fish.

The kids join hands.

The ducks swim.

then	went
sleep	pick
three	see
right	night
light	be
black	green

LESSON **56**

56.1 Silent E Machine

	tap		pin
	can		cub
	cap		rid
	hop		cut
	kit		hat
	rob		mad
	rip		rat
	tub		rod

56.1 Silent E Machine continued

e

e

e

e

e

e

e

e

e

e

e

e

e

e

e

e

LESSON 57

Name _____

57.1 Phonogram Bingo

ee	ch	igh
er	wh	oi
ay	ai	oy

sh	th	ai
oy	ay	oi
ch	er	igh

cap	cape
hat	hate
cane	can
robe	rob
bit	bite
note	not

past	paste
slide	slid
plan	plane
scrape	scrap

Name _____

K k *K k*

K

K

K

K

ropes ___   tent ___

wheels ___   gas can ___

clubs ___   box ___

net ___   tail light ___

poles ___   flag ___

LESSON 58

Name _____

58.1 Uppercase V

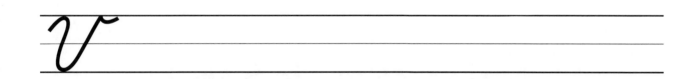

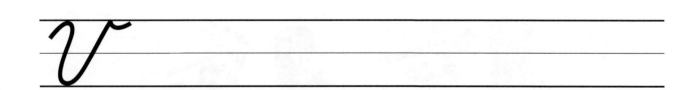

Which bike is hers?

The pink bike with black wheels is hers.

Which chair is hers?

The green chair is hers.

Which cake is his?

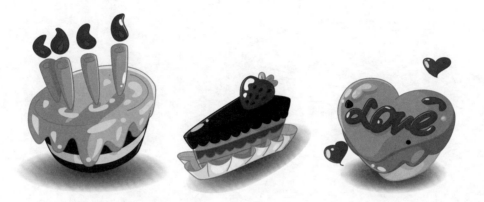

The cake with a green top and red flames is his.

Which plane is his?

The white plane is his.

tap	tape
can	cane
cap	cape
glob	globe
hop	hope
kit	kite
rob	robe
slid	slide
past	paste

58.3 Silent E Game

Silent E Words	Silent E Words
Silent E Words	Silent E Words
Silent E Words	Silent E Words
Silent E Words	Silent E Words
Silent E Words	Silent E Words
Silent E Words	Silent E Words
Silent E Words	Silent E Words
Silent E Words	Silent E Words
Silent E Words	Silent E Words

LESSON 59

Name _____

59.1 Uppercase Y

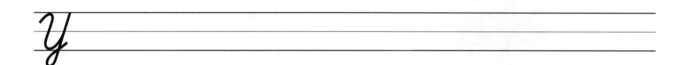

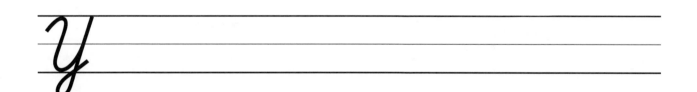

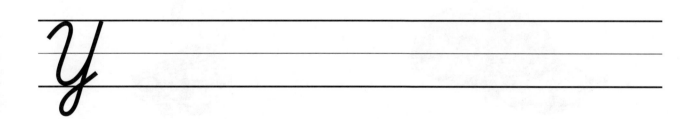

cub__

cub__

pin__

pin__

cap__

cap__

pin	pine
cub	cube
rid	ride
while	gate
gap	sale
store	rack
rake	track
bike	fire
cake	sack

59.3 Silent E Game

Silent E Words	Silent E Words
Silent E Words	Silent E Words
Silent E Words	Silent E Words
Silent E Words	Silent E Words
Silent E Words	Silent E Words
Silent E Words	Silent E Words
Silent E Words	Silent E Words
Silent E Words	Silent E Words
Silent E Words	Silent E Words

The man has a rake.

The kids like the cake.

She jumps in the pile.

The man is on the pole.

He digs a deep hole.

He rode the bike.

She has a big smile.

LESSON 60

Name _____

60.1 Uppercase C

C

C

C

C

____ing

____ing

____ing

____ing

_____ong

____ing

r

k

sw

s

str

str

ay	oy	ee	wh
ck	er	oi	igh
th	ng	s	qu
sh	ai	ch	y

60.3 Phonogram Bingo continued

ch	wh	qu	igh
th	ay	s	ee
ai	ng	er	y
sh	ck	oy	oi

REVIEW D

D.1 Initial Sounds

___oy

___oy

tr

d

b

r

c

t

___ake

___ake

___uck

___uck

Name _____

R W U I J

1. | sh | oy | wh | ch |

2. | ai | u | o | oi |

3. | ee | ai | sh | ay |

4. | oy | igh | ai | wh |

5. | n | ng | m | igh |

6. ay   ai   oy   oi

7. sh   er   igh   ee

Which fish is his?

His fish has five black stripes.

Which toy is hers?

Her toy has a string. It is a kite.

Which ship is his?

His ship is not green or red. His ship has a white sail.

Which pet is hers?

Her pet is not a dog. Her pet is green. It is a snake.

LESSON **61**

61.1 Uppercase E

$\mathcal{E}$

$\mathcal{E}$

$\mathcal{E}$

$\mathcal{E}$

1. E   e   F   I   C   e   N   E

2. U   Y   Y   O   y   y   z

3. J   j   j   y   T   G   t   g

4. i   l   e   n   I   i   m   t

5. M   n   M   m   N   m   n

6. R   B   P   p   p   r   r   R

61.3 Silent E's

_____
_____
_____

_____
_____
_____

_____
_____
_____

_____
_____
_____

_____
_____
_____

_____
_____
_____

61.3 Silent E's continued

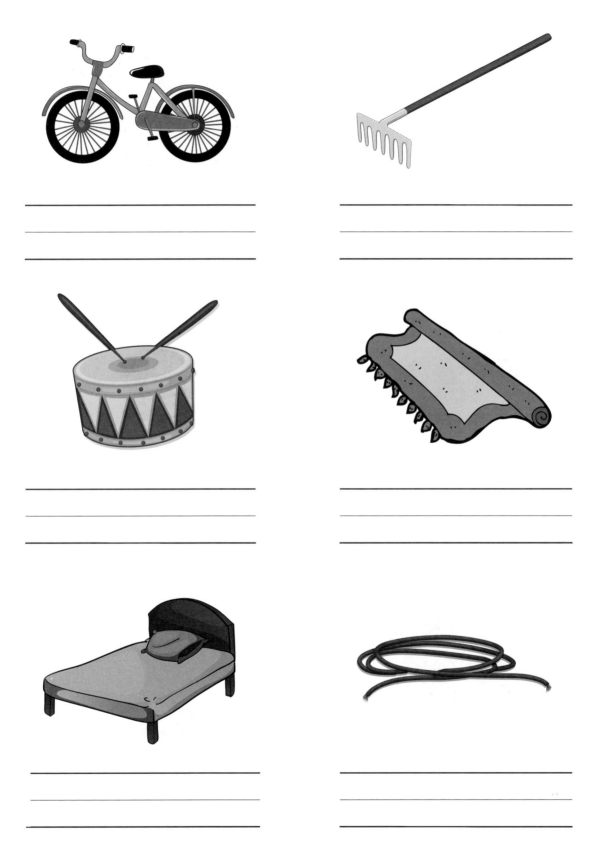

61.3 Silent E's continued

kite	bike
hat	hive
cake	sun
mop	rake
drum	rug
bed	rope

Silent E Words

Silent E Words

Silent E Words

Silent E Words

Silent E Words

Silent E Words

Silent E Words

Silent E Words

Silent E Words

Silent E Words

Silent E Words

Silent E Words

LESSON 62

Name _____

62.1 Uppercase O

O

O

O

O

The man in the hat has a cake.

He has a big cone.

He broke his kite.

The man tugs on the mule.

The boy dove in the lake.

The bees chase the man.

He stands on a globe.

LESSON **63**

Name _____

63.1 Uppercase Q

Q

Q

Q

Q

63.2 Charades

box	boy
cake	car
farm	fire
game	home
love	pig
rain	ring
sing	stand
street	time
toy	wind

63.2 Charades continued

High Frequency Words

High Frequency Words

High Frequency Words

High Frequency Words

High Frequency Words

High Frequency Words

High Frequency Words

High Frequency Words

High Frequency Words

High Frequency Words

High Frequency Words

High Frequency Words

High Frequency Words

High Frequency Words

High Frequency Words

High Frequency Words

High Frequency Words

High Frequency Words

LESSON 64

Name _____

64.1 Uppercase G

$\mathcal{G}$

$\mathcal{G}$

$\mathcal{G}$

$\mathcal{G}$

make

date

man

fling

He plays a drum.

He digs a hole.

He rides a bike.

He gets the mail.

He drives a car.

He paints with blue paint.

He jumps up high.

He gets a big gift.

He plays a tune on his sax.

He drives a ship.

He lights a lamp with a stick.

He sleeps at his desk.

LESSON 65

Name _____

65.1 Phonogram Bingo

or	ee	ai	igh
ck	ar	er	oi
wh	ay	ng	sh
a	th	oy	u

er	th	ck	or
ai	sh	wh	oy
ar	u	ee	ng
oi	ay	ch	igh

frog

truck

star

tire

tree

REVIEW

E.1 Silent Final E

tap	tape
rat	rate
bite	bit
globe	glob
cut	cute

Name _____

$\mathcal{E}$ $\mathcal{O}$ $\mathcal{Q}$ $\mathcal{G}$

1.   r   oy   or   ar

2.   ng   m   th   wh

3.   ar   ay   ai   or

The cat has a blue fish.

The boy with a blue top and black shorts has a big cone.

Sam and Kate go on a hike.

The man sees a clue.

Mom and Dad ride the bike.

Lots of fish chase the big blue fish.

LESSON 66

Name _____

66.1 Uppercase L

$\mathcal{L}$

$\mathcal{L}$

$\mathcal{L}$

$\mathcal{L}$

am	wash
as	want
of	blue
bring	but
came	can
chair	corn
day	far
five	for

High Frequency Words

High Frequency Words

High Frequency Words

High Frequency Words

High Frequency Words

High Frequency Words

High Frequency Words

High Frequency Words

High Frequency Words

High Frequency Words

High Frequency Words

High Frequency Words

High Frequency Words

High Frequency Words

High Frequency Words

High Frequency Words

High Frequency Words

High Frequency Words

LESSON 67

67.1 Uppercase X

𝓧

𝓧

𝓧

𝓧

bluff

cliff

fluff

huff

off

puff

gave	get
give	got
had	has
have	her
here	him
high	hot
his	off
2	2
4	4

High Frequency Words

High Frequency Words

High Frequency Words

High Frequency Words

High Frequency Words

High Frequency Words

High Frequency Words

High Frequency Words

High Frequency Words

High Frequency Words

High Frequency Words

High Frequency Words

High Frequency Words

High Frequency Words

High Frequency Words

High Frequency Words

High Frequency Words

High Frequency Words

LESSON **68**

68.1 Uppercase Z

ä	ē	ā	ĕ
ō	ĭ	ö	ŭ
ū	ŏ	ü	ă

68.3 Spelling Mystery

fall	ball
tall	wall
mall	call
bell	sell
well	tell

Mystery	Mystery
Mystery	Mystery
Mystery	Mystery
Mystery	Mystery
Mystery	Mystery

will	well
its	way
when	like
live	long
do	made
make	may
name	nine
which	week
Trap!	**Trap!**

High Frequency Words

High Frequency Words

High Frequency Words

High Frequency Words

High Frequency Words

High Frequency Words

High Frequency Words

High Frequency Words

High Frequency Words

High Frequency Words

High Frequency Words

High Frequency Words

High Frequency Words

High Frequency Words

High Frequency Words

High Frequency Words

High Frequency Words

High Frequency Words

LESSON 69

Name _____

69.1 Long, Short, and Broad Vowels

ă	ŏ
ĕ	ä
ö	ē
ā	ō
ū	ŭ

mess

less

miss

moss

toss

glass

grass

all	ball
full	call
full	fall
doll	hill
pull	class
grass	or
pink	push
put	quit

High Frequency Words

High Frequency Words

High Frequency Words

High Frequency Words

High Frequency Words

High Frequency Words

High Frequency Words

High Frequency Words

High Frequency Words

High Frequency Words

High Frequency Words

High Frequency Words

High Frequency Words

High Frequency Words

High Frequency Words

High Frequency Words

High Frequency Words

High Frequency Words

The boy made a big mess.

1. Sam has the ball.

2. Sam will kick the ball to Tom.

3. Tom will pass the ball to Rob.

4. Rob will kick the ball to Mat.

5. Mat will pass the ball to Mac.

6. Mac will bump the ball.

Name _____

Sam

Mat

Mac

Rob

Tom

LESSON 70

70.1 Rhyming

fat	miss
hiss	will
sit	cat
hill	fit

day	clue
live	tall
true	jar
ball	play
star	give

Name _____

Did Zack take the white ball?

add	odd
egg	mutt
mitt	buzz
fuzz	fizz
whizz	jazz

Mystery	Mystery
Mystery	Mystery
Mystery	Mystery
Mystery	Mystery
Mystery	Mystery

those	us
ride	use
white	say
want	to
small	song
start	ate
take	tell
these	thing
Put back 2 cards	**Put back 2 cards**

High Frequency Words

High Frequency Words

High Frequency Words

High Frequency Words

High Frequency Words

High Frequency Words

High Frequency Words

High Frequency Words

High Frequency Words

High Frequency Words

High Frequency Words

High Frequency Words

High Frequency Words

High Frequency Words

High Frequency Words

High Frequency Words

High Frequency Words

High Frequency Words

REVIEW **F**

F.1 Short, Long, and Broad Vowels

E.2 Handwriting

Name _____

1. | sh | th | wh | ar |

2. | igh | ay | or | ai |

3. | ar | or | oi | igh |

4. | th | wh | or | ar |

5. | n | sh | m | ng |

The bell on the clock will ring.

The pup will ride her bike.

The pup will push the cart with eggs and a duck on top.

She will take a bath with her duck.

The pup will push his cart full of bones with a ball on top.

The pup will hang up a star.

She will make a wish.

The pup will take a call.

Name _____

these   take

small   ride

push   when

ball   long

white   name

put   which

LESSON 71

71.1 Tic-Tac-Toe

tch	or	ar
ng	ai	oi
ay	oy	wh

igh	oy	ar
or	ch	tch
th	wh	ai

71.1 Tic-Tac-Toe continued

ch	tch	wh
th	sh	ai
oi	ay	oy

ck	ee	er
wh	tch	ar
ch	or	ay

___atch

___atch

w

h

scr

str

c

m

___etch

____atch

___atch

___atch

Name _____

Rose wants to play a game with Luke.

Ring the bell.

Sing a song.

Put on the shorts.

Put on a hat.

Sit on the chair.

Take off the hat.

Stand up.

Put on the watch.

Clap six times.

Ring the bell.

Ring the bell.

Put on a hat.

Clap three times.

Kick the ball.

Smile big.

Drink the glass of water.

Take off the hat.

Pet the dog.

Put the rug on the chair.

Sit on the chair.

Ring the bell.

Ring the bell.

Jump three times.

Put on the shorts.

Sit on the chair.

Hug the dog.

Stand on the rug.

Put the fork on the chair.

Toss the ball.

Catch the ball.

Push the car.

Ring the bell.

Ring the bell.

Put on a hat.

Jump six times.

Push the car.

Sit on the rug.

Stand up.

Put the chair on the rug.

Put the dog on the chair.

Put the shorts on the chair.

Take off the hat.

Ring the bell.

LESSON 72

72.1 OW Words

cow	bow
how	now
brown	clown
snow	mow
grow	low
town	wow
blow	row
show	bowl

ow Words

ow Words

ow Words

ow Words

ow Words

ow Words

ow Words

ow Words

ow Words

ow Words

ow Words

ow Words

ow Words

ow Words

ow Words

ow Words

The crowd at the game cheers.

The sun glows in town. A red car drives on the street.

The stars shine. The tent glows in the night.

Sam has on a red life vest. He rows.

The boy throws the trash in the green can.

Mom, Dad, and the kids shop in town while the snow falls down.

She blows her nose.

The clown smiles and throws the balls.

Name _____

light	go
tall	dark
stop	thick
thin	short
black	slow
fast	white

Sheep has a big day. He wakes up on his back. Then he blows his nose and takes a bath. He sips a cup of milk.

Sheep puts his hands on his hips and thinks. He plays a horn and plays his flute.

For lunch sheep has a cake. His mom gives him a gift. He jumps with joy.

Then he takes his pole to the lake to catch a fish.

At the end of the day, sheep sleeps.

72.4 Sheep continued

Throw the ball and Sam will catch it.

LESSON 73

Name _____

73.1 Matching

She sits on a branch up high in the tree. Her dad calls to her.

She put bugs that make light in the jar.

She has a crown. She sings a song.

He has on a red mask and a red cape.

She hugs her dad. She rides on his back.

She rides with her mom in the blue truck.

Name _____

you	she	he	it
to	a	me	say
for	down	can	has
when	do	I	round

What is your name?

LESSON 74

74.1 OUGH Words

Dad bought a new bike.

He has a bad cough.

They fought about the game.

Though it was late, I did not want to go home.

We drove through the rain.

She thought we left at six.

I am round.
You hit me with
sticks or pound
on me with your
hands. I am loud.
What am I?

I make a sound.
I wake him up. I
have a bell. I tick.
What am I?

I grow on a tree.
I am sour. I am
green. What am I?

We bought a blue bike at the store.

LESSON 75

Name _____

75.1 Syllables

1 2 3

1 2 3

1 2 3

1 2 3

1 2 3

1 2 3

Name _____

clown_

cow_

bell_

cake_

star_

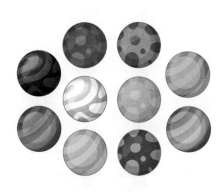

ball_

All three help mix the dough.

REVIEW G

G.1 Plurals

snail_

light_

rope_

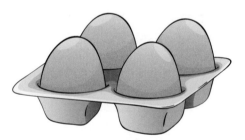

egg_

cloud_

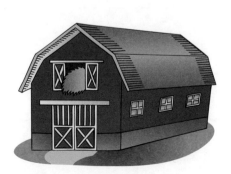

barn_

The brown cow laid down on the grass.

1. ch tch ou igh

2. ough ou oy f

3. ou or tch wh

4. oy ay ar ow

The cow is black with white spots.

It tastes quite sour.

That is a black crow.

Watch him throw the ball.

The pink, green, and blue
fish is a trout.

He had a thought.

She has a bad cough.

Pam and her mom made
the dough for the rolls.

She likes to help her
mom make soup.

use	say
to	thing
start	week
your	well
fall	I
ate	you

LESSON 76

Name _____

76.1 Rhymes

frown	late
now	fought
skate	how
dress	town
thought	mess

I thought it was a fun show.

"Run fast," said Tom.

"Have fun," said Mom.

Dad said, "Pick up your socks."

The dog barks, "Yip, yip, yip."

The kids yell, "Help! Help!"

"Wait next to the chair," said Mom.

"Pass the ball to me," said the kid.

"Beep, beep," rang the clock.

"I need a drink," said the small boy.

"I want more jam," said Sam.

"Here is your box," said the clerk.

76.3 Reading Quotes

Quotes

Quotes

Quotes

Quotes

Quotes

Quotes

Quotes

Quotes

Quotes

Quotes

Quotes

LESSON 77

pay	paid
pays	lay
laid	lays
say	said
says	

77.1 Find It! continued

Find it! Find it!

Find it! Find it!

Find it! Find it!

Find it! Find it!

Find it! Find it!

"Do you want a drink?"

"I do not feel well. I have a bad cough."

"Help! What is that thing?"

"I have on a bright vest and hat so that cars can see me on the street."

"I need to go to bed. I need more sleep."

"I want to win this game."

watch	snow
out	what
thought	said
says	was
round	I
you	your
down	brown
count	found
grow	how

High Frequency Words

High Frequency Words

High Frequency Words

High Frequency Words

High Frequency Words

High Frequency Words

High Frequency Words

High Frequency Words

High Frequency Words

High Frequency Words

High Frequency Words

High Frequency Words

High Frequency Words

High Frequency Words

High Frequency Words

High Frequency Words

High Frequency Words

High Frequency Words

77.4 Handwriting   **Name** _____

Mom said, "Do not fight with him."

LESSON 78

78.1 Spelling Mystery

by	my
sky	dry
try	fry
fly	shy
spy	why

Name _____

pain	ball
try	lane
doll	bees
rich	high
these	more
for	pitch

Jack has the ball. He runs down the court. He throws the ball to Zack.

Zack throws the ball to Jim.

Jim stands. He sees Nate. He throws the ball to Nate.

Nate gets the ball. He runs down the court.

He throws the ball to Jon.

Jon makes a jump shot.

Tom gets the ball off the rim.

Jack

Tom

Zack

Jon

Nate

Jim

Jill said, "I have to be home by six."

LESSON 79

79.1 The Phonogram EA

Take your **seat**.

He hit his **head**.

We had a **great** day.

Did you **clean** the sink?

The cow **eats** grass.

fight	lane
bead	late
do	seed
grain	white
sigh	through
great	my

Name _____

We will eat bread for lunch.

LESSON 80

80.1 Making New Words

c		t
cr		st
fl	oa	k
g		l
s		p

young	why
warm	try
own	our
now	my
ate	by
fly	show
boat	coat
eat	read
head	bread

High Frequency Words

High Frequency Words

High Frequency Words

High Frequency Words

High Frequency Words

High Frequency Words

High Frequency Words

High Frequency Words

High Frequency Words

High Frequency Words

High Frequency Words

High Frequency Words

High Frequency Words

High Frequency Words

High Frequency Words

High Frequency Words

High Frequency Words

High Frequency Words

"What a great game!" said the coach.

REVIEW

Name _____

H.1 Rhyming

leg

dock

tall

lake

Tom said, "We won the game!"

1. or   ea   oa   ar

2. igh   tch   ough   ch

3. ee   ai   ow   ea

4. oa   ou   ough   ay

5. | ou | oa | ea | or |

6. | ow | ea | ough | oa |

The boat sails on the lake at night

The plane is up high in the sky.

I think the red team will win the match.

We like to read by the
big oak tree.

We like to read at
the beach.

We like to eat cones
at the beach.

We like to play games
by the tree.

says	why
said	coat
now	bread
our	grow
own	brown
try	count

Foundations
Logic of English®

LEVEL **B**

Kimber Iverson

Fred the Frog

Reader 1

That Fred!
He is a fun frog!

6

This is Fred.
He is a frog.

1

He thinks he
can get a tan.

Fred thinks he
is not a frog.

He thinks he can
go on a fast trip.

4

Fred thinks
he is a kid.

3

Reader 2

Max

Foundations
Logic of English

LEVEL **B**

Kimber Iverson

Then he chomps
on greens.
Crunch, crunch!

6

Max needs lunch.

1

Max sighs.

He peeks at a duck.

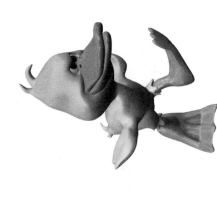

The duck quacks
and flees.

4

He might creep
up and get it.

3

Foundations
Logic of English

LEVEL B

Kimber Iverson
Libby Johnson

Toys Play!

Reader 3

"At last we can play!
Join me, toys!"

6

The clock ticks.
The toys wait.

1

Foundations Level B - Reader 3

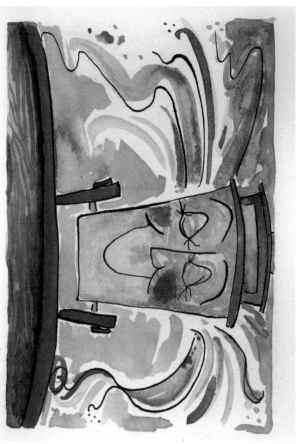

The train grins with joy.

5

Foundations Level B - Reader 3

The sun sets and it is night. The toys wait.

2

But when the boy
sleeps, the toys perk up!

The boy lays in bed.
The toys wait.

Foundations

Logic of English®

B LEVEL

Kimber Iverson

Reader 4

Can Pete
Pick a Pet?

Pete likes this pet best!

6

Pete might get a pet. Which pet is the right pet?

1

But this pet can play
games with Pete and
doze on his lap.

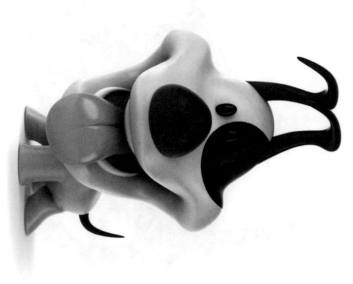

This pet can ride a bike.

This pet can dive
in a lake.

4

This pet can skate.

3

Reader 5

Quite a Farm!

Foundations

Logic of English®

LEVEL **B**

Kimber Iverson

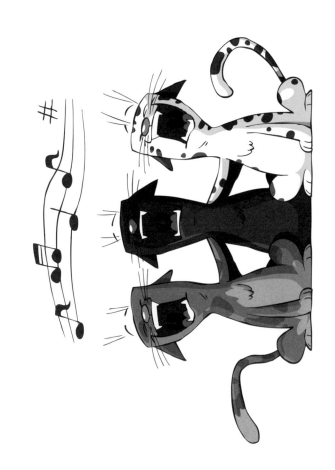

The cats can sing
a tune. Jake has
quite a farm!

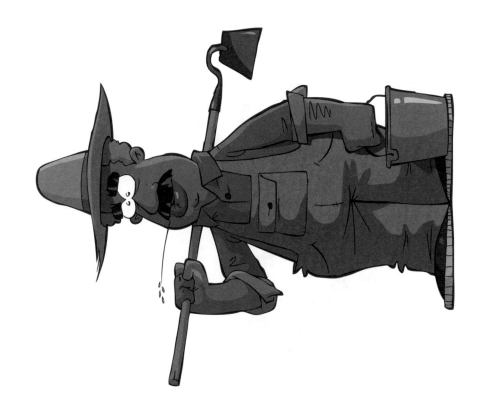

Jake lives on a farm.

The pig can get a ride.

He has a smart bunch
on his farm.

These hens lay pink, blue, and green eggs.

4

This hen can make a sock.

3

Foundations
Logic of English®

LEVEL B

Kimber Iverson

Reader 6

Kids Just Want to Have Fun

These kids just want
to make a mess!

6

Mark wants
to be a plane.

1

Jeff wants to go give
his mom a wet hug.

Jane wants
to tell a joke.

Sue wants to play hide and seek.

4

Lee wants to feel the wind.

3

Reader 7

Time to Bake

Foundations
Logic of English®
LEVEL B

Kimber Iverson

Yum! Kate wants
to make more!

6

Liz sifts the flour.

1

All three help
mix the dough.

Kate and Liz watch while
Meg pours the milk.

Kate gets the right
egg and cracks it.

4

Meg gets an egg. But
this is not the right egg!

3

Reader 8

My Best Game

Foundations
Logic of English®
LEVEL **B**

Kimber Iverson

"We won!"
our team cheers.
What a great game!

Our team is red. When
the game starts, we
run back and forth and
chase the ball.

It is a goal! Score!

The blue team plays well. It is a tough game.

Yes! The ball makes it!

8

All of us play hard,
but no balls go
through the goal.

3

7

The ball soars through the air. Will it make it?

4

"Try to score!" yells my coach. Will the time run out?

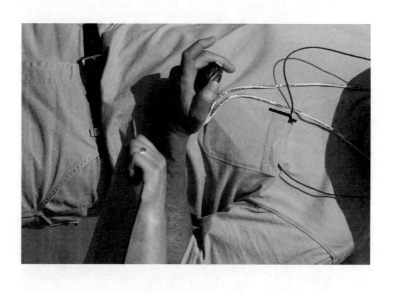

I run and kick it.

6

Now I see the ball
close to me.

5